WEARING GLASSES

BY HARRIET BRUNDLE

KidHaven PUBLISHING

HUMAN BODY HELPERS

OPTOMETRIST

Published in 2019 by
KidHaven Publishing, an Imprint of Greenhaven Publishing, LLC
353 3rd Avenue
Suite 255
New York, NY 10010

Designer: Danielle Rippengill
Editor: Kirsty Holmes

Photo credits: *All images are courtesy of Shutterstock.com, unless
otherwise specified. With thanks to Getty Images, Thinkstock Photo
and iStockphoto. Front Cover & 1 – Beatriz Gascon J, NikaMooni, Milan
M. Images used on every spread – Beatriz Gascon J, NikaMooni, yana
shypova. 2 – Visual Generation, Jane Kelly, inithings. 5 – Filip Dokladal.
7 – kidstudio852. 8 – thailerderden10. 9 – natrot, Stock_VectorSale,
mayrum. 10 – ByEmo. 11 – edel. 12 & 13 – jehsomwang. 14 – Dezay,
Macrovector. 15 – svtdesign. 16 – E.Druzhinina. 18 – Iuliia Saenkova. 19
– Visual Generation, Jane Kelly, inithings. 20 – ElkhatiebVector, Mix3r. 22 –
nawamin, Katrin FTZ. 23 – Igdeeva Alena.*

All facts, statistics, web addresses and URLs in this book were verified
as valid and accurate at time of writing. No responsibility for any
changes to external websites or references can be accepted by either
the author or publisher.

Cataloging-in-Publication Data

Names: Brundle, Harriet.
Title: Wearing glasses / Harriet Brundle.
Description: New York : KidHaven Publishing, 2019. | Series: Human
body helpers | Includes glossary and index.
Identifiers: ISBN 9781534529472 (pbk.) | ISBN 9781534529496 (library
bound) | ISBN 9781534529489 (6 pack) | ISBN 9781534529502
(ebook)
Subjects: LCSH: Eyeglasses–Juvenile literature. | Vision disorders–
Juvenile literature. | Eye–Examination–Juvenile literature.
Classification: LCC RE976.B77 2019 | DDC 617.7'522–dc23

Printed in the United States of America

CPSIA compliance information: Batch #BW19KL: For further information contact Greenhaven
Publishing LLC, New York, New York at 1-844-317-7404.

Please visit our website, www.greenhavenpublishing.com. For a free
color catalog of all our high-quality books, call toll free 1-844-317-7404
or fax 1-844-317-7405.

CONTENTS

Words that look like **this** can be found in the glossary on page 24.

YOUR EYES

EYES ... WE ALL HAVE THEM. BUT WHY DO WE NEED THEM?

Our eyes are always sending messages to our brain, helping us to see the world around us.

Our two eyes work together to make a **3-D** picture of what we are seeing, telling us information like how far away something is or its color.

There are lots of different parts to our eyes and they work together to help us to see. **Eyesight** differs, so yours might be different from someone in your family, or from your friends.

WHAT ARE GLASSES?

GLASSES ARE USED TO HELP US TO SEE MORE CLEARLY.

Glasses have lenses, which are pieces of glass or plastic that are made especially to help our **vision**.

Hi! I'm Lucy Lens and I'm here to help make your sight perfect.

As you get older, the lenses in your glasses may change.

Each person with glasses has lenses that are exactly right to help their eyes. A pair of glasses that helps one person might not make a difference for another, or could even make their vision worse.

Wearing the wrong lenses might make you feel a bit strange!

GLASSES HAVE FRAMES, WHICH HOLD THE LENSES IN PLACE.

Glasses have frames to hold the lenses, arms to loop over your ears, and ear and nose pieces to make your glasses feel more **comfortable** and keep them from sliding off.

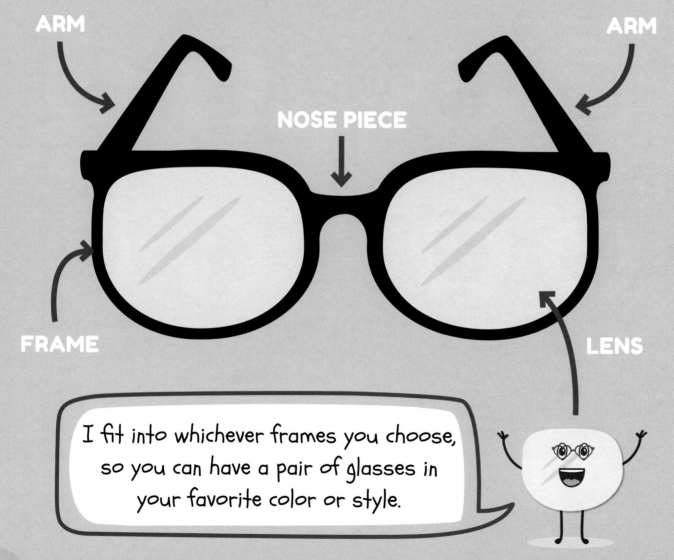

ARM

ARM

NOSE PIECE

FRAME

LENS

I fit into whichever frames you choose, so you can have a pair of glasses in your favorite color or style.

When you have your glasses fitted, these parts will be made to fit your face perfectly.

It's important that your glasses sit correctly.

WHY MIGHT I NEED GLASSES?

You might need glasses because you are nearsighted, which is also known as myopia. If you are nearsighted, things in the distance are not clear.

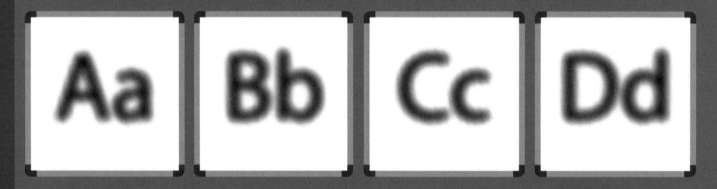

You might notice road signs and the board at school are tricky to read and look a bit **blurry**.

You could need glasses because you are farsighted, which is also known as hyperopia. This means that things close to you are not clear. You might find that reading or writing is difficult.

You could have astigmatism. This means your eye is egg-shaped rather than round and can make your vision blurry.

HOW DO GLASSES WORK?

Our eyes use light to send our brain the messages it needs to see the things around us. If your vision is not clear, it's because light is hitting your eyes in the wrong place and it needs to be corrected.

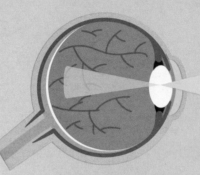

MYOPIA

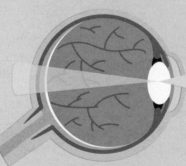

HYPEROPIA

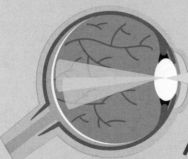

ASTIGMATISM

That's where I come in!

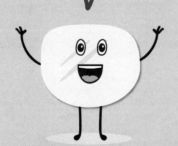

The lenses in a pair of glasses bend the light to make it hit exactly the right part of the eye. When the light hits the correct place, it makes our vision as clear as possible.

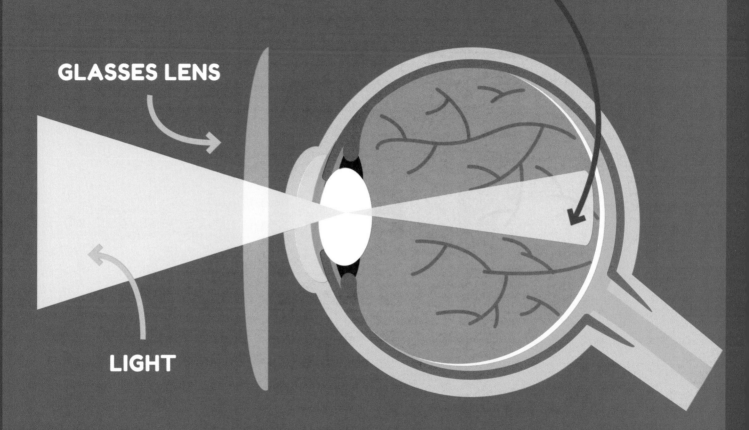

GLASSES LENS

LIGHT

You won't be able to notice it happening and you can't feel it, either.

WHAT HAPPENS AT THE OPTOMETRIST?

When you go to see the **optometrist**, they will test your eyes in different ways to check how well you can see and that your eyes are healthy.

Your **appointment** won't take long and doesn't hurt a bit!

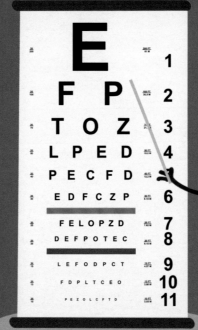

OPTOMETRIST

They may ask you to read out lines of letters of different sizes or shine a light into your eyes.

If your optometrist decides you need glasses, they will give you a **prescription**, which tells you the strength your lenses need to be.

Hi, my name is Lucy.

Hi, Lucy! My name is Ernie.

+3
PRESCRIPTION

Now for the fun part! You can pick out your frames, and within a few days your glasses will be ready.

WHAT TO EXPECT

When you first put your glasses on, you should notice that your vision is clearer.

Wow! What a difference a pair of glasses can make!

You should be able to see everything perfectly, especially anything that seemed blurry before you had your glasses.

For the first few days you might feel aware of your glasses on your face, or be able to notice the frames around your eyes.

Don't worry, Ernie, it won't be long before you're used to me being here.

Don't worry, after a while you'll become used to the feeling of wearing your glasses.

DOS AND DON'TS

DO take good care of your glasses. Make sure you keep them inside a case when you're not wearing them so the lenses don't get scratched.

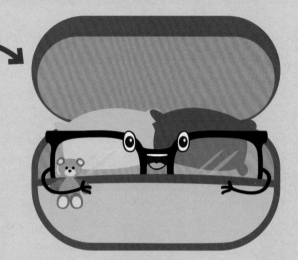

DON'T leave your glasses lying around where they could get damaged.

Please make sure you take good care of me – I don't want to get damaged!

DO make sure that you go to each of your appointments with the optometrist so they can check that you are wearing the right prescription and your eyes are healthy.

OPTOMETRIST

If you feel your glasses don't fit correctly or aren't helping, be sure to tell an adult.

LIFE WITH GLASSES

Once you start wearing your glasses, you might need to be more careful when playing sports.

If you're worried about playing sports with glasses, tell your teacher or parent.

If you can't manage without your glasses, try to be extra careful with anything that could hit your face.

YOU MIGHT NOTICE THAT WEARING GLASSES IN THE RAIN CAN BE A BIT OF A PAIN!

Don't panic, inside your glasses case there is usually a small cloth that can be used to clean the water off your glasses.

BYE BYE GLASSES!

AS YOU GET OLDER, YOUR OPTOMETRIST MAY OFFER YOU THE CHANCE TO TRY CONTACT LENSES.

These are small, round lenses that you place **<u>directly</u>** onto your eyeball. Wearing contact lenses means you won't need to wear your glasses all the time.

You must take contact lenses out after you have worn them for the **recommended** amount of time.

We won't see each other every day now, but I'll still be here when you need me.

Don't worry, Lucy. We'll still see each other.

LEFT

RIGHT

You could have contact lenses that you clean and use again or ones that you throw away each day.

GLOSSARY

3-D	an image with depth
APPOINTMENT	meeting someone at a place or time
BLURRY	not clear
COMFORTABLE	give a pleasant feeling
DIRECTLY	nothing in between
EYESIGHT	the ability to see
OPTOMETRIST	a person who can say if you need glasses or contact lenses and check eye health
PRESCRIPTION	a piece of paper that shows exactly which lenses you need
RECOMMENDED	how something should be done
VISION	the ability to see

INDEX

7